Rhodesian Ridgebacks

Lyn Sirota
and
Maria Koran

MEDIA ENHANCED BOOKS
AV2 BY WEIGL
ADDED VALUE • AUDIO VISUAL
www.av2books.com

AV^2 provides enriched content that supplements and complements this book. Weigl's AV^2 books strive to create inspired learning and engage young minds in a total learning experience.

Go to **www.av2books.com**, and enter this book's unique code.

BOOK CODE

A989348

AV^2 by Weigl brings you media enhanced books that support active learning.

Your AV^2 Media Enhanced books come alive with...

Audio
Listen to sections of the book read aloud.

Key Words
Study vocabulary, and complete a matching word activity.

Video
Watch informative video clips.

Quizzes
Test your knowledge.

Embedded Weblinks
Gain additional information for research.

Slide Show
View images and captions, and prepare a presentation.

Try This!
Complete activities and hands-on experiments.

... and much, much more!

Published by AV^2 by Weigl
350 5th Avenue, 59th Floor
New York, NY 10118
Website: www.av2books.com

Library of Congress Cataloging-in-Publication Data

Names: Sirota, Lyn A., 1963- , author. | Koran, Maria, author.
Title: Rhodesian ridgebacks / Lyn Sirota, Maria Koran.
Description: New York, NY : AV2 by Weigl, 2016. | Series: All about dogs | Includes index.
Identifiers: LCCN 2016052090 (print) | LCCN 2016052657 (ebook) | ISBN 9781489656148 (hard cover : alk. paper) | ISBN 9781489656155 (soft cover : alk. paper) | ISBN 9781489656162 (Multi-user ebk.)
Subjects: LCSH: Rhodesian ridgeback--Juvenile literature.
Classification: LCC SF429.R5 S57 2016 (print) | LCC SF429.R5 (ebook) | DDC 636.753/6--dc23
LC record available at https://lccn.loc.gov/2016052090

Printed in the United States of America in Brainerd, Minnesota
1 2 3 4 5 6 7 8 9 0 20 19 18 17 16

122016
120116

Project Coordinator: John Willis Art Director: Terry Paulhus

Weigl acknowledges Getty Images, iStock, Shutterstock, Minden, and Alamy as its primary image suppliers for this title.

All About Dogs

Rhodesian Ridgebacks

Contents

Name That Dog

What dog has a ridge of hair down its back?

What dog can jump over tall fences?

What big dog comes from Africa?

What dog was once used in packs to hunt lions?

There is only one answer...

The Rhodesian ridgeback!

African Lion Hound

Ridgebacks come from an area of Africa that was once known as Rhodesia. They are a mix of African and European dogs. European farmers, who arrived in Africa in the 1500s, had brought dog **breeds** such as danes, mastiffs, greyhounds, bloodhounds, and terriers with them.

The farmers needed a dog that was well-suited to life in Africa. It had to be able to help protect them and their farms. This dog needed to be able to survive in the African bush.

Today, Rhodesia is now the countries Zambia and Zimbabwe.

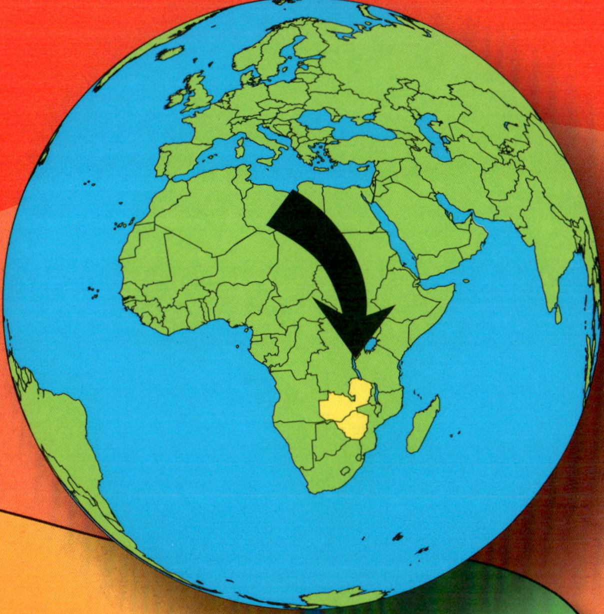

The Khoikhoi people of Africa had dogs known for ridges of hair along their backs. Over time, these dogs had puppies with the European dogs. The puppies had **features** of both the European and the African dogs, including the ridge. These dogs were strong and loyal. They became known as Rhodesian ridgebacks.

Ridgebacks kept cattle safe from large animals. Farmers used them to hunt fierce cats, such as lions. This is why ridgebacks are sometimes called African lion hounds.

In 1922, Rhodesian ridgeback owners set a **standard** for the breed. This let people know which dogs were true Rhodesian ridgebacks. People first brought ridgebacks to the United States in 1950. In 1955, the breed was recognized by the American Kennel Club (AKC). This made ridgebacks an official breed of dog in the United States.

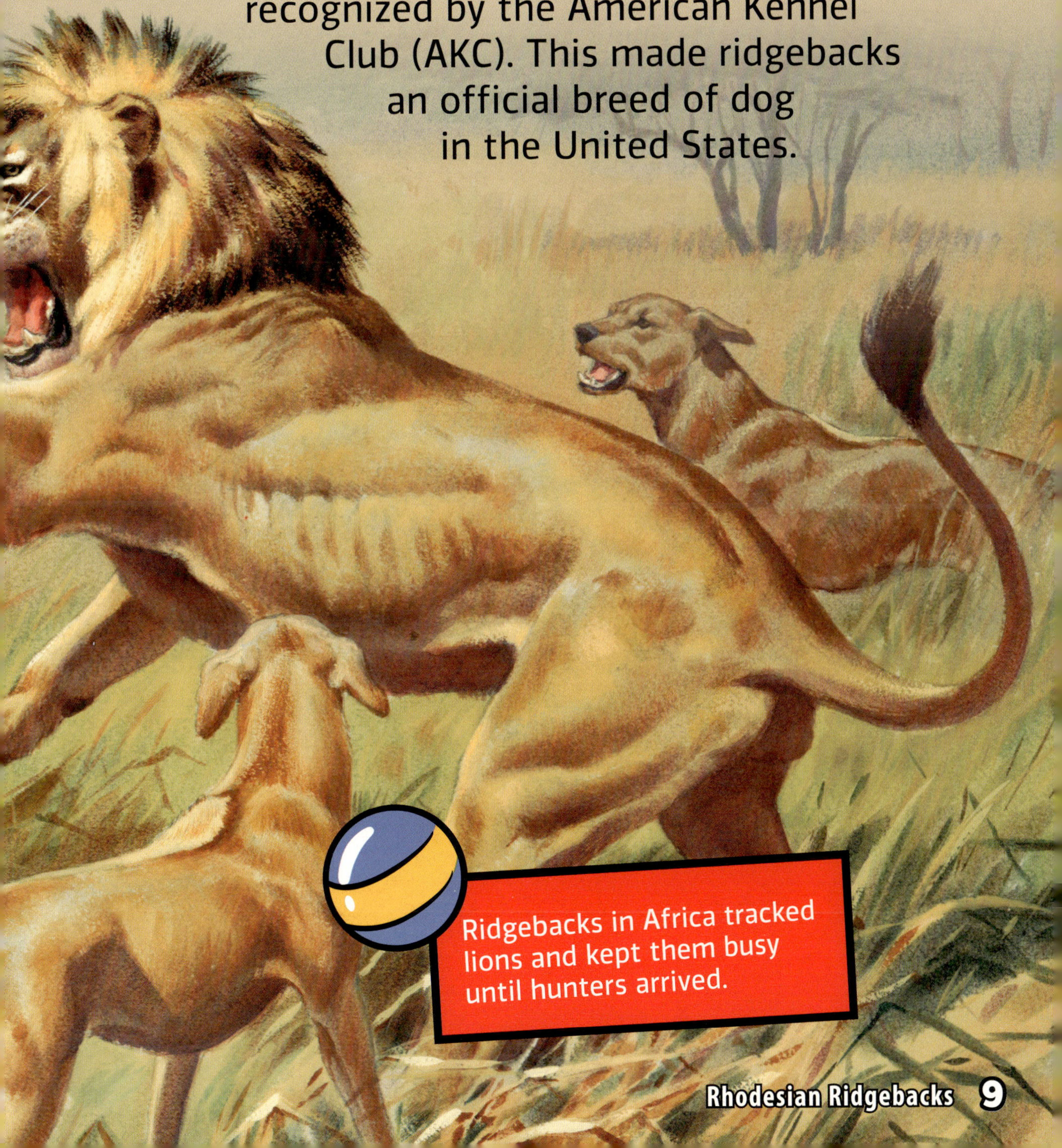

Ridgebacks in Africa tracked lions and kept them busy until hunters arrived.

Ridgebacks are clean dogs. Their coat does not smell, and they do not shed very much.

The Ridge

At a glance, ridgebacks have a very regal appearance. Their long, elegant necks hold a powerful head. These dogs can have black or brown noses. Black-nosed ridgebacks may have a dark muzzle. This feature makes them look like they are wearing a mask. A ridgeback's ears are wide, with round tips. Although ridgebacks appear fearless, they also look friendly and sweet.

Ridgebacks have short, shiny hair. These dogs are wheaten, or reddish-brown, in color. Some have white markings on their chests and toes. Their height ranges from 24 to 27 inches (61 to 69 centimeters). An adult ridgeback can weigh between 64 and 90 pounds (29 and 41 kilograms).

The two identical curls at the beginning of a ridgeback's ridge are called crowns or whorls.

The Rhodesian ridgeback is the national dog of South Africa.

The ridge that the breed gets its name from is formed by its back hairs. These hairs grow along a ridgeback's spine in the opposite direction of the rest of its coat. The ridge begins behind the dog's shoulders, and reaches to about its hips.

Rhodesian ridgebacks have strong, sturdy legs. Ridgebacks have **compact** paws, and their toes are **arched**. These dogs have tough, round pads on their feet. The pads protect their toes from rough ground and thorns.

Ridgebacks have fairly long tails. Their tails are thick at the base and come to a point. A ridgeback's tail has a slight upward curve.

Most Rhodesian ridgebacks have ridges with matching sides.

Power Hound

Rhodesian ridgebacks are powerful hounds. Their strong muscles and lungs allow them to trot for a long time. Ridgebacks can run faster than most humans can sprint. Although ridgebacks can swim, they are not fond of water.

Getting exercise and staying busy is important for a Rhodesian ridgeback's happiness and health. A ridgeback needs something to do, or it may develop unwanted behaviors. A bored ridgeback will wander off on its own in search of small animals, such as squirrels or rabbits. It may dig large holes in a yard.

Rhodesian ridgebacks have a top speed of 20 miles (32 kilometers) per hour.

A ridgeback should be at least one year old before it takes part in activities such as agility training or racing.

An adult Rhodesian ridgeback can jump over a 5-foot (1.5-meter) fence.

Ridgebacks have calm **personalities** and do not often get excited. Ridgebacks are loving and good with families. They will protect their masters.

Rhodesian ridgebacks are smart dogs. Training them in a firm, positive way is key. They make great hunting partners. Ridgebacks have a strong protective **instinct**, so they do not need to be trained as watch dogs. That behavior comes naturally to them.

Ridgebacks want to be loved. They are affectionate dogs that crave family time. They can be distant with new people. Ridgebacks need to be introduced to people and other animals at a young age. Familiar dogs and cats are good playmates for them.

Ridgeback Puppies

Rhodesian ridgeback mothers often have about 6 to 10 puppies, but a **litter** may include more than 15. Puppies have thicker coats than adults. Many will shed or lose part of their fur as they get older.

With good food and exercise, Ridgeback puppies can more than double their weight in as little as two months. They reach their adult size when they are about 14 months old. Young ridgebacks are very active, but become calmer and quieter as they age.

Ridgeback puppies are born with their ridges.

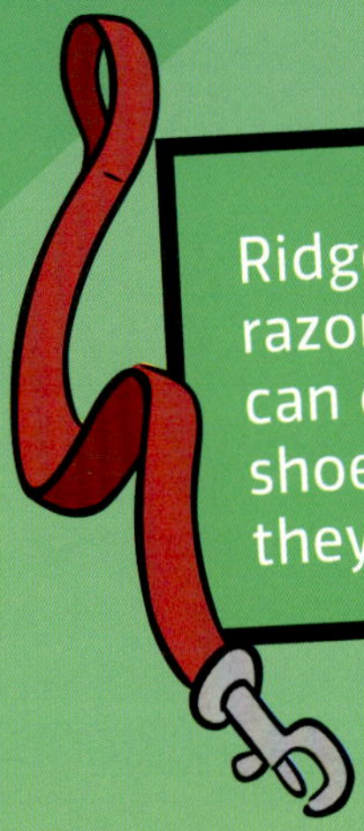

Ridgeback puppies have razor-sharp teeth. They can destroy wood tables, shoes, and anything else they can get their paws on.

Ridgeback pups are not picky eaters. They will eat just about anything they can reach. Careful feeding with special dog food at set times is important. Human food should be kept away from ridgebacks, as they are known to get into cupboards and onto counter tops in search of a meal.

Ridgeback puppies need love, attention, space, and training. Ridgebacks must be kept on leashes when they are being walked. They should be watched closely to keep them safe. A ridgeback should not be left on its own for long periods of time. Ridgebacks need a yard with a sturdy fence that is at least 6 feet (1.8 m) tall.

Ridgeback puppies should eat three meals a day until they are 12 to 14 weeks old. Older puppies should be given two meals each day.

Ridgebacks were bred to track other animals without being heard.

Work and Play

Ridgebacks have helped hunters for many years. Today, few ridgebacks work as hunting dogs. Most are family pets, and others help people in different ways.

The Lion Dog Group was formed in South Africa. This group uses ridgebacks as working dogs. The dogs help find large animals for tourists to watch. They also warn their owners of dangerous snakes and wild pigs.

Rhodesian ridgebacks are usually very quiet dogs. However, if working ridgebacks find an animal, they make a **rumble** deep in their chests. This is like sounding an alarm.

The AKC first organized lure coursing trials in 1991. Ridgebacks were accepted as competitors one year later.

Today, many ridgebacks take part in **lure** coursing. Dogs compete in this sport by chasing after a quickly-moving lure. The lure may be made of plastic or artificial fur.

Lure coursing allows ridgebacks to express their strong hunting drive while keeping themselves and other animals safe. The dogs are scored based on their speed, endurance, and how well they follow after the lure as it twists and turns. Organizations such as the American Sighthound Field Association (ASFA) operate hundreds of coursing events each year.

Ridgebacks have a great sense of smell, but rely on their eyes to help hunters find prey. This makes the breed a type of "sight hound."

A Rhodesian ridgeback needs at least two hours of exercise each day.

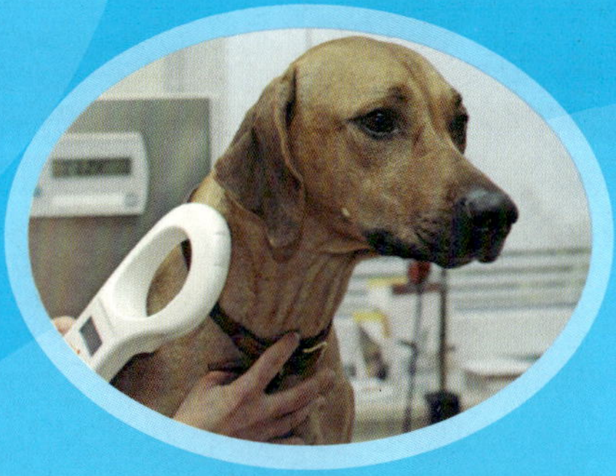

Caring for a Ridgeback

As a breed, ridgebacks are most suitable for experienced dog owners. Understanding more about the breed will help people know if a ridgeback is the right dog for them. Ridgebacks can be strong, smart, and stubborn. They need to be trained from a young age.

Rhodesian ridgebacks need to walk, run, and play. A ridgeback's owner can keep it busy by taking it on hikes. Ridgebacks should not be kept outside all of the time. A blend of being outside and inside works well for them.

Taking good care of a ridgeback costs money. An owner needs to plan for costs such as food, toys, leashes, collars, beds, and training.

Ridgebacks do not need special grooming. A bath or wipe down once a week will keep them clean. The points of their nails should be cut or filed one or two times each month. Their teeth should be brushed daily. A gentle cleaning of their ears each week helps with wax buildup.

Most ridgebacks are healthy dogs. However, sometimes they can develop health problems. Areas to watch are their hips and eyes. A good breeder or **veterinarian** can answer an owner's questions and concerns. With love and care, a ridgeback may live for 10 to 12 years.

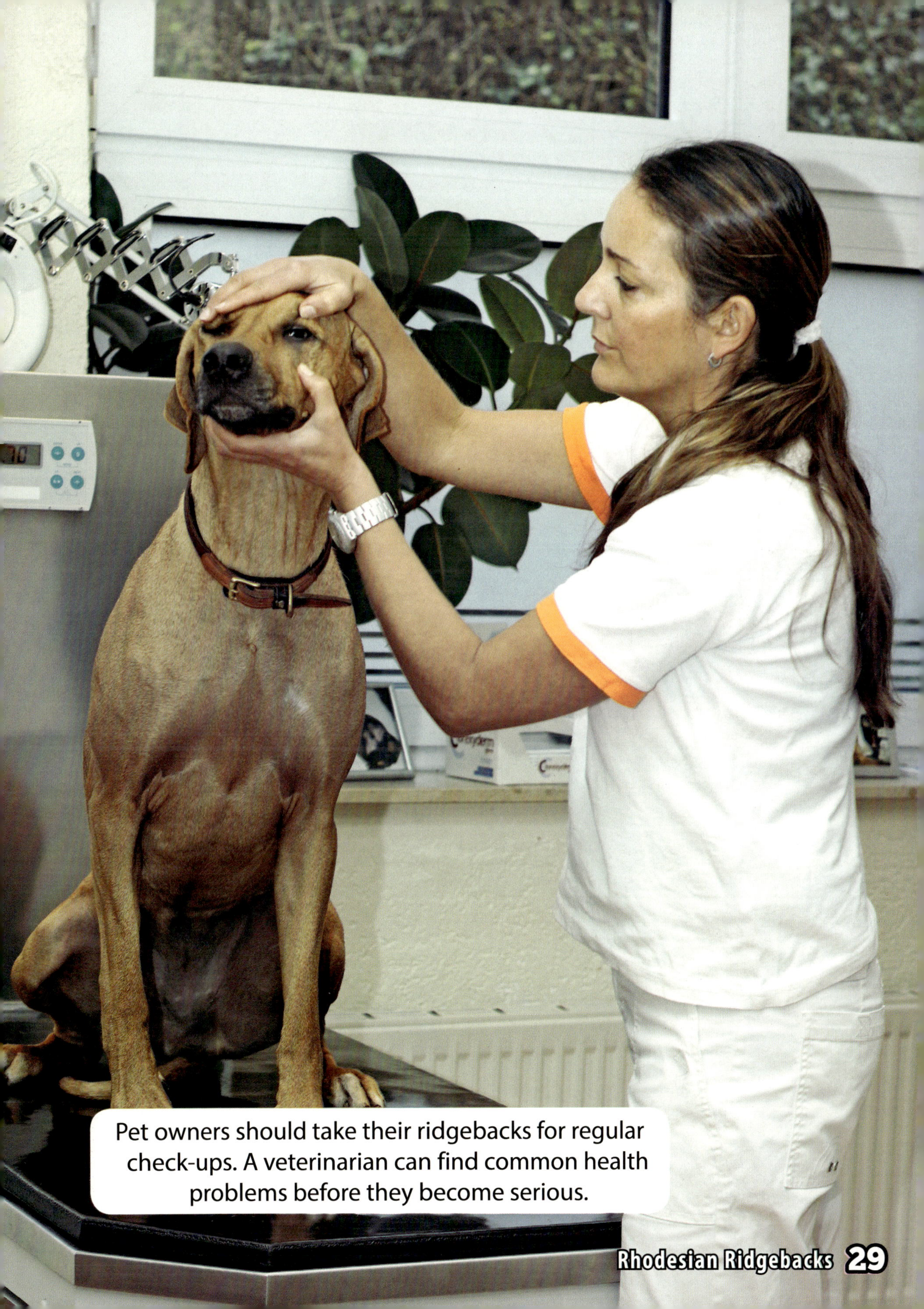

Pet owners should take their ridgebacks for regular check-ups. A veterinarian can find common health problems before they become serious.

Rhodesian Ridgeback Quiz

Q: How long do ridgebacks usually live?

A: 10 to 12 years

Q: When did the AKC organize its first lure coursing trial?

A: 1991

Q: At what age does a ridgeback reach its adult size?

A: 14 months

Q: What is another name people call Rhodesian ridgebacks?

A: African lion hounds

Q: What is a Ridgeback's ridge made out of?

A: Hair

Q: Where is the Rhodesian Ridgeback breed originally from?

A: Rhodesia, now known as Zambia and Zimbabwe

Key Words

arched (AHRCHT): forming a curve

breeds (BREEDS): types of animals that are different from other members of their species

compact (kahm-PAKT): closely packed together

features (FEE-chur): interesting or important parts of something

instinct (in-STINGKT): a natural pattern of behavior

litter (LIH-tur): a group of babies born to one animal at the same time

lure (LOOR): something used to attract animals

personalities (pur-suh-NAL-i-tees): qualities that form character

rumble (RUHM-buhl): a deep sound

standard (stan-DARD): a level of quality that something should meet

veterinarian (vet-rih-NAIR-ee-uhn): a person who treats injured or diseased animals

Index

Log on to www.av2books.com

AV² by Weigl brings you media enhanced books that support active learning. Go to www.av2books.com, and enter the special code found on page 2 of this book. You will gain access to enriched and enhanced content that supplements and complements this book. Content includes video, audio, weblinks, quizzes, a slide show, and activities.

AV² Online Navigation

Audio
Listen to sections of the book read aloud.

Book Pages
AV² pages directly correspond to pages in the book.

Video
Watch informative video clips.

Key Words
Study vocabulary, and complete a matching word activity.

Embedded Weblinks
Gain additional information for research.

Quizzes
Test your knowledge.

Slide Show
View images and captions, and prepare a presentation.

Try This!
Complete activities and hands-on experiments.

AV² was built to bridge the gap between print and digital. We encourage you to tell us what you like and what you want to see in the future.

Sign up to be an AV² Ambassador at www.av2books.com/ambassador.

Due to the dynamic nature of the Internet, some of the URLs and activities provided as part of AV² by Weigl may have changed or ceased to exist. AV² by Weigl accepts no responsibility for any such changes. All media enhanced books are regularly monitored to update addresses and sites in a timely manner. Contact AV² by Weigl at 1-866-649-3445 or av2books@weigl.com with any questions, comments, or feedback.